How Money is Coined:

A Visit to the United States Mint, New Orleans

WITH INTRODUCTION BY

GREG LAMBOUSY
DIRECTOR OF COLLECTIONS,
LOUISIANA STATE MUSEUM

UNIVERSITY OF LOUISIANA AT LAFAYETTE PRESS
2009

ISBN: 1-887366-89-X

University of Louisiana at Lafayette Press
University of Louisiana at Lafayette
P.O. Box 40831
Lafayette, LA 70504-0831

http://cls.louisiana.edu

For more information on the Louisiana State Museum, visit:
http://lsm.crt.state.la.us/

The United States Mint, New Orleans

by Greg Lambousy,
Director of Collections, Louisiana State Museum

Coining operations began in the New Orleans Mint facility in 1838, though the building was not actually completed until 1839. It became the only mint to produce a Confederate coinage when the Confederate States of America occupied it in April of 1861. Following Reconstruction minting was resumed in 1879, but by 1909 the operation had become obsolete and was superseded by new mints in San Francisco and Denver. The assay office, however, continued during much of Reconstruction and did not cease operations in the building until 1931 when the office was moved to the New Orleans Customhouse on Canal Street.

On March 3, 1835 President Andrew Jackson, the hero of the Battle of New Orleans, signed a bill authorizing the U. S. Treasury to establish a branch mint in New Orleans. By the same act, branch mints were also established in Charlotte, North Carolina and Dahlonega, Georgia. The Southern branch mints were the result of Andrew Jackson's long war with the Bank of America and paper currency. New Orleans was selected as a location for the manufacture of hard currency because it was the "emporium of the Great Valley" with gold specie from Mexico flowing through its active markets.

Gibson's Guide and Directory of the State of Louisiana and the Cities of New Orleans and Lafayette (1838) describes the Mint building as

> . . . situated on what was formerly called Jackson Square, being nearly the former site of Fort St. Charles and was designed by Wm. Strickland, architect, and contracted for by John Mitchell and Benj. F. Fox, builders. It is an edifice of the ionic order, of brick, plastered to imitate granite; having a center building projecting, as also two wings, is strongly built, with very thick walls and well finished . . . The total length of the edifice is 282 feet, and the depth about 180—the wings being 29 by 81, and the whole three stories in height. It was begun September 1835, and is now on the point of being completed—at a cost of 182,000 . . . The Square is being surrounded by a neat iron railing on a granite basement.

Congress authorized the New Orleans Branch Mint to produce coinage of gold and silver. The 1838 "O" mark dime was the first coin produced. Circulating gold coinage was initiated the following year with a low volume of quarter eagles. By the middle of the 1850s, the New Orleans Branch Mint was producing in silver: dollars, half dollars, quarter dollars, dimes, half dimes, and three cent pieces. In gold coinage, the Mint produced double eagles, eagles, half eagles, three-dollar pieces, quarter eagles, and dollars.

The basic processes involved in coining United States currency remained relatively unchanged throughout the operational history of the New Orleans Branch Mint. A number of guidebooks covering coining operations at the New Orleans Mint and the parent Mint in Philadelphia were published in the nineteenth century. The earliest publication dealing with New Orleans operations, besides general regulations issued by the Mint itself, was a small pamphlet by John Leonard Riddell first printed in 1845 entitled *The Mint at New Orleans with an Account of the Process of Coinage.* (This pamphlet was also printed in *DeBow's Review* and again in the 1960s by numismatist Eric P. Newman.) Later, in 1880 a guide incorporating and enlarging on Riddell's account was published as *A Brief Description of the United States Mint: A Brief History of the Mint with the Modus Operandi by which Silver and Gold are Converted into Money and Other Interesting Matter.* The *New Orleans Daily Picayune* published a rather in-depth, illustrated article on operations at the mint in 1891 entitled "Making Money: A Visit to One of the Most Interesting Places in New Orleans, The United States Branch Mint." Author Farran Zerbe quotes from a lost 1895 publication on the New Orleans Mint entitled simply "History of the Mint" in his June, 1905 article from the *Numismatist* magazine. Perhaps the most comprehensive guidebook was published by E. S. Gardner in 1897 as *How Money is Coined: A Visit to the United States Mint, New Orleans.* Gardner apparently spent some time at the Mint and took a number of wonderful photographs illustrating key aspects of the coining process. The copy of *How Money is Coined* now in the library of the Louisiana State Museum was originally owned by one of the women who worked in the adjusting department.

Operations were divided into four separate departments: treasury, melting and refining, assaying, and coining. The treasurer received all bullion brought to the Mint for coining. He also was charged with safeguarding the bullion and coin in the mint before and after being sent to the other departments. The melter and refiner was responsible for creating gold and silver ingots of the proper fineness from raw bullion. Samples of the melter and refiner's work were tested by the assayer to insure that the correct combinations of precious metals and alloys were employed. The coiner received the approved ingots from the melter and refiner. After passing the ingots through rollers, they were next drawn through an apparatus that reduced them to the proper thickness from which blanks could be punched. The blanks (or planchets) were then checked for accuracy of weight and cleaned. Any underweight planchets were returned to the melter and refiner. After being milled, so that a ridge was raised around the edge of the planchet, it was sent to the pressing room to receive the impression of its respective denomination and ultimately transferred back to the treasurer.

The New Orleans Mint received gold and silver principally in the form of dust, bars, foreign coin, and old jewelry. A fee was charged for the expense of refining or toughening the metal, if so required. All bullion was weighed in the presence of the treasurer, the foreman of deposits, and the depositor. The weigher gave the owner a receipt for the actual weight of the deposit and forwarded the bullion to the melting department by way of the custodian of the bullion vaults. After being melted and cast into a bar, two samples were taken by the treasurer and delivered to the assayer. Each sample or "assay-slip" was then rolled until flat and a piece clipped away, wrapped in lead foil with a gram of pure silver and placed in a cupel. Receptacles made of bone-ash, cuples were heated at high temperatures in a furnace with the metal to be assayed. After heating, the base metals were absorbed by the pores of the cuple, leaving a button of pure gold or silver.

If silver remained, it was analyzed further by a process termed the "humid assay" which involved the use of various chemicals for determining the purity of silver. If the assay was of gold, the gold was melted with silver about three times its own weight. Then, the alloy was rolled into a thin coil or "cornet" and subjected to repeated doses of nitric acid—the acid removed the silver, leaving only the gold. The remaining metal was washed, dried, and annealed at a high temperature, then weighed and the proportion of gold arrived at. The assayer estimated the value of the bullion and called upon the treasurer to pay the amount to the depositor, minus the fee for assaying, after returning all bullion remaining from the operations of the assay to the treasurer After four days had passed, the depositor could submit his receipt to the register and receive in return a warrant for the amount due in US currency. The cashier would then pay the depositor after receiving the warrant.

The process of separating and purifying the bullion took place on the basement floor. Deposits composed of a mixture of gold and silver and other metals required separation. When purifying gold a certain amount of pure silver was added, then the whole emersed in nitric acid. The gold was unaffected by the acid but the silver was completely dissolved. After drawing off the silver solution, the gold was then gathered in a pan and washed. The impurities mixed with silver were removed by the use of nitric acid. The silver along with the base metals were reduced to a liquid form. The liquid was then run through a series of tubs. Saltwater was added and the solution thickened. By adding zinc, virgin silver formed while the base metals remained in a liquid state and were discarded.

When bullion of known value was delivered to the Mint it was debited to the melter and refiner who processed the bullion into ingots for the coiner. When, as mentioned previously, the purity of the bullion was uncertain, a "deposit melt" was conducted. In this process, the bullion was rendered homogeneous so that a representative sample could be taken from the melt for assay. In theory, each deposit was treated separately and never mixed.

The melting room was located on the second or principal floor of the building. It contained all of the apparatus for creating gold and silver ingots. Large furnaces held graphite crucibles containing bullion. Distilled coal (coke) was ignited under the vessels in an enclosed chamber beneath a raised platform. A metal lid on the top of each furnace was moved by means of a cantilevered hoist, which was hand operated. Up to 8,600 ounces of bullion could be placed in a crucible and the crucible set into the furnace for melting. Borax was added to the heated crucible as a fluxing agent to increase cohesion of the melt. The crucible was generally left in the furnace for forty minutes while an attendant intermittently skimmed the dross from the top. Once the metal reached the right temperature, a pair of tongs was used to remove the crucible from the furnace and pour the molten metal into the molds. The rotary ingot machine located on a grated platform in front of the large furnaces held the molds. A stream of cold water circulated through the machine to cool the molten metal.

The finished ingots were given over to the coiner in specific allotments to be sent first to the rolling room. Bullion was transferred between departments on carts by piling specially designed boxes one on top of the other and covering them with a fitted piece of sheet metal that was in turn strapped to the cart by a locked chain. One end of the ingot was wedge-shaped to allow for passing through the rolling machine. The rollers were calibrated to a prescribed dimension to more closely match the width required for the specific coinage. Ingots were passed through the rolling machine to reduce the metal to a thickness required for the particular coin being produced. After passing through the rollers a number of times the metal took on a spring-like temper and was annealed in a furnace contained in the same room at various points throughout the process. By altering the space between the rollers the desired thickness for the strip could be attained. After rolling, the strip was usually six times its original length or six feet long.

The drawing bench finished the work of the rolling machine. Strips of gold or silver were literally drawn between small steel cylinders. The space between the cylinders was precisely calibrated to produce a strip the exact thickness needed for cutting planchets. One end of the strip was made thinner than the other to allow it to run between the cylinders. A powerful set of pencers connected to a carriage that ran along the length of the bench, fastened itself to the strip and pulled it through the cylinders. In this way, a highly uniform strip was created. From these strips of bullion discs slightly larger than the coins to be made were cut.

The cutting presses consisted of a vertical steel punch. One cutting press could cut two hundred and twenty-five planchets per minute at full speed. The perforated strips were sent back to be remelted along with any obviously defective planchets. The remaining planchets were next transferred to the adjusting department for further sorting.

From 1879 until the closing of the New Orleans Mint in 1909 women were employed in the adjusting room where they separated "light" from "heavy" planchets. Generally, in the 19th century, employers believed females were best suited for the delicate and detailed filing work required in the adjusting room. As such, women predominated in this department. At that time, women had already found employment in these capacities at the Philadelphia Mint and other mints in England, France, India and several South American nations. As early as 1852, the New Orleans Mint coiner, A. Devall requested that women be employed in the adjusting department as they were being employed in Philadelphia.

Using very sensitive balances, the women determined if the planchets weighed within the limit of acceptability. If a planchet weighed less than it should, the planchet was condemned and returned to the melting department. If the planchet weighed more than it should, the excess was filed off of the edge, or condemned, if too excessive for filing. This filing was a very delicate procedure and demanded a certain amount of dexterity and patience. The women were seated close to the table so that a leather apron with one end tacked to the table and the other end fastened under their arms would catch any falling gold or silver. The windows often remained closed—even during summer months—to prevent air currents from blowing the dust generated by filing and disturbing the delicate scales.

A *New Orleans Daily Picayune* reporter described the adjusting room in 1891:

> The adjusters are seated at long tables, each one with her balance and implements before her and several pans of money at hand. The balances are of the most delicate sort of mechanism, so finely made that a breath of wind will disturb the correct weighing of the money, and for this reason the windows and doors are kept closely shut during working hours, the only air in the room entering through ventilators and gauze wire doors opening on the gallery; but even these must be closed if the breeze blows too strongly, and then one may imagine what it is in that room---thirty-nine people breathing the same impure air and inhaling the poisonous silver dust into their lungs, to say nothing of the heat of a mustard poultice intensity; but fortunately it does not often happen that all of these ventilators have to be closed at one time, and the coiner and the assistant coiner are very lenient in allowing the doors and windows to be opened at frequent intervals during the day, so as to air the room during the heated term.

The planchets that passed inspection were next sent to the milling room on the third floor. The milling machine created a raised edge on the planchets. Several planchets were placed in vertical brass tubes at once. Each tube, located along the outer top portion of the machine, was designed for different sized coins. The planchets were fed into a groove between a revolving steel wheel and stationary wall. The wheel rotated the planchet against itself and the wall four times before it exited the machine. In this way the edge of the planchet was raised to a prescribed height. Milling was done to prevent wear to the surface of the coin and to allow for ease of stacking. Approximately five to twelve hundred planchets could be milled within a minute's time depending on the denomination.

After milling the planchets they were then annealed. The planchets were placed in the annealing furnace and heated to high temperatures, then dipped in a solution of boiling sulfuric acid. This process adjusted the planchet's temper to the desired hardness and cleaned the coins' surface of any impurities. The planchets were dipped in cold water to remove the acid and then placed in the drying machine, where sawdust was used to absorb the water. Sawdust, loose metal, and other foreign matter were removed by rolling the planchets in the revolving riddle machine. After cleaning, the planchets were transferred to the pressroom on the second floor.

Women operators generally attended the coining presses after 1879. In the coining room there were several presses used to coin various denominations. There were two presses dedicated to silver dollars, one for the half dollar, one for the quarter dollar, and one for the dime. Planchets were "fed" to the press by the attendant. The planchets were placed in a brass tube from which steel feeders grasped the planchet and deposited it into a collar between the dies. The dies were prepared by the parent Mint in Philadelphia and sent to the various branches as needed. As the dies closed on the planchet with the force of 150 tons, the feeders returned for another planchet. The pressure of the dies compressing the planchet forced the metal into the fluted edges of the collar—creating a "reeding" effect on the rim of the coin. When the feeders grasped the next planchet, they also lifted the coin from between the dies. As the feeders moved forward they deposited the next planchet between the dies and released the coin into a hamper. Stamping in this manner, the presses averaged eighty-five coins a minute.

The coins were then returned to the adjusting room where they were reviewed for proper weight and appearance. They were then sent to the weigh room. The coins were weighed in bulk on large bullion scales and counted. These scales were capable of weighing from 5,000 ounces to one grain. An even mixture of "light" and "heavy" coins were used to constitute a "delivery". This mixture allowed for reducing or increasing the weight of the delivery in fractional increments. Wooden counting boards contained copper partitions, the particular height and width of the number of coins to be counted. After the board was filled, the coins were slid into a box and ready for delivery. The superintendent was notified of the completed delivery and it was weighed again in the presence of the treasurer. If the weight was within acceptable limits, then the delivery was placed in a vault. Samples from the delivery were sent to the assay department in Philadelphia (and later, Washington, DC). If the samples met requirements, then the whole delivery was ready for circulation pending orders from the Sub-treasury. If, however, the samples did not meet requirements, then the whole delivery was condemned and re-melted.

In 1922, a supervising architect for the Treasury Department issued a report describing the general decay into which the building and its remaining machinery had fallen:

> ...The attic and building generally contains old decayed tanks, masonry furnaces, old iron, piles of paper, mud and dead pipe and gas lines and flues, etc., and many holes in masonry floor arches exist without any apparent reason. Surface dirt and cobwebs exist practically throughout the building, the accumulation of years, and there is no janitor force employed. The rear lot and courtyard is filthy with trash, cans, old abandoned machinery, decayed and falling wooden and sheet metal sheds and shacks and an old brick chimney.

At this time in 1922 the assay department was still operating on the third floor of the building. A Naval Recruiting Station, a Veterans Bureau dispensary and dental clinic operated in other parts of the building. The architect recommended in his report that the assay department relocate to the New Orleans Customhouse, where it could share the use of a newly built bullion vault. His advice was finally taken in 1931 when the Mint building was converted into a federal prison. In 1943 the prison closed. The building functioned as a Coast Guard Receiving Station until the middle 1960s when it was transferred from the Federal Government to the State of Louisiana and placed under the stewardship of the Louisiana State Museum Board. The mint opened to the public as a part of the Louisiana State Museum complex in 1979.

HOW MONEY IS COINED.

ILLUSTRATED.

A VISIT TO THE UNITED STATES MINT, NEW ORLEANS.

Published by
E. S. GARDNER,
Des Moines, Iowa.

Introduction.

IT IS SAFE to assume that any American citizen could name the different coins now in common circulation in the United States. We are all familiar with the silver dollar and the smaller coins called fractional currency. Thousands of dollars in coin pass from hand to hand daily in the ordinary transactions of business; and yet, a surprisingly large majority of our people cannot describe correctly even the inscriptions on these familiar coins. Let the reason for this lack of knowledge be what it may, the fact remains, and strongly suggests that there is room in the public mind for enlightenment on this subject.

In offering this little book to the general public, it is with the hope and belief that it will be welcomed as a source of reliable information, free from political speculations, and presenting only the facts relating directly to the operations of coinage. In the arrangement of the within illustrations and descriptive matter, I have tried to reproduce the scenes and impressions which characterize an actual trip through the Mint. So that those who have never seen the reality may here find a true reflection of it. And to those whose privilege it has been to visit the Mint, may it prove to be an acceptable souvenir.

It is with pleasure and appreciation that I here acknowledge the kindly interest taken in this work by the Superintendent of the Mint, Mr. Overton Cade, and his assistants, but for whose courtesy it would not have been possible to secure the illustrations and facts herewith presented. E. S. G.

1. UNITED STATES MINT, NEW ORLEANS, LA.

THERE are four Mints operated by the United States Government. They are located at Philadelphia, Pa., New Orleans, La., Carson City, Nev., and San Francisco, Cal. The building shown in our first illustration is the home of the New Orleans Mint, which, with its grounds, occupies a block frontage on Esplanade Avenue, near the levee.

On first entering this building, my attention was attracted by the large double engine near the center of a space not far beyond the main entrance. The working of this engine, together with the general noise and a perceptible jar to the floor, impresses one that powerful operations of some kind are in progress, and that there is no play about making money, even here.

Visitors are required to register at the desk, near the entrance, before they are permitted to begin their tour of inspection. Having complied with this regulation, our little party was taken in charge by the chief conductor, who proceeded to show and explain to us the various operations of the Mint. With but a few minor and unimportant exceptions, all coins are made in the same manner; so, let us take for an example, the Silver Dollar, and follow it on its journey of evolution.

2. SILVER BULLION.

We were first conducted to the room where silver and copper bullion is stored, and weighed preparatory to melting.

At the far end of the room are huge scales capable of weighing from 10,000 ounces down to 1–100 of an ounce. By the side wall were piled bricks of silver bullion. (Plate 2.) These bricks each weigh on an average 1,200 ounces, Troy. They are 999–1000, pure, and there is enough silver in each one to make over 1,500 silver dollars.

Out of curiosity I measured one of them, and here are the figures: 11½ inches long, 5½ inches wide, and 3¾ inches high. Pure silver being too soft to withstand the wear which coins receive in circulation, 10 per cent of copper is added to give sufficient hardness. Standard coin silver contains 900 parts of pure silver and 100 parts of pure copper. In adjusting the proportion of the metals preparatory to melting, great care must be exercised; for only *one and one-half thousandths* variation is allowed on either side of the standard, "900 fine." That is, if, after melting, the assayer's test shows the proportion to be 2–10 of a milligram *less* than 898½ parts of pure silver in 1,000, the lot is condemned. It must be re-melted and enough pure silver added to bring the fineness within the variation limit. Should the test show 2–10 of a milligram *more* than 901½ parts of pure silver, the lot is also condemned and more copper must be added.

3. MELTING ROOM.

For melting, the bullion is placed in a large crucible which is then set into a furnace and surrounded with a coke fire. About 8,600 ounces of bullion are placed in the crucible at one time, and this quantity constitutes what is called a "melt."

When the metals become sufficiently heated in the furnace, the attendant stirs and mixes the molten mass thoroughly, so that the proportion of fineness will be evenly distributed. When the melted metal is ready, it is poured into moulds which form it into ingots. At the beginning of this pouring process, a little of the metal is dropped into a cup of ice-water, which granulates the silver. This is then taken to the assayer who tests the silver for fineness. Three different tests are made in this way,—at the beginning, midway, and at the end of the pouring. This is done to guard against any error in assaying (as the tests should agree)—and also to prove that the ingots are all of even quality, and of the proper fineness.

Let us refer for a moment to Plate 3. On the left are buckets of coke which is the fuel used in the furnaces. Beyond the coke are small furnaces used to test small lots of silver and gold which are to be purchased by the Mint. The large furnaces on the raised platform are used for melting bullion. Above and behind the left hand furnace is one of the crucibles in which are placed the metals to be melted. Between the furnaces on the platform is the machine which

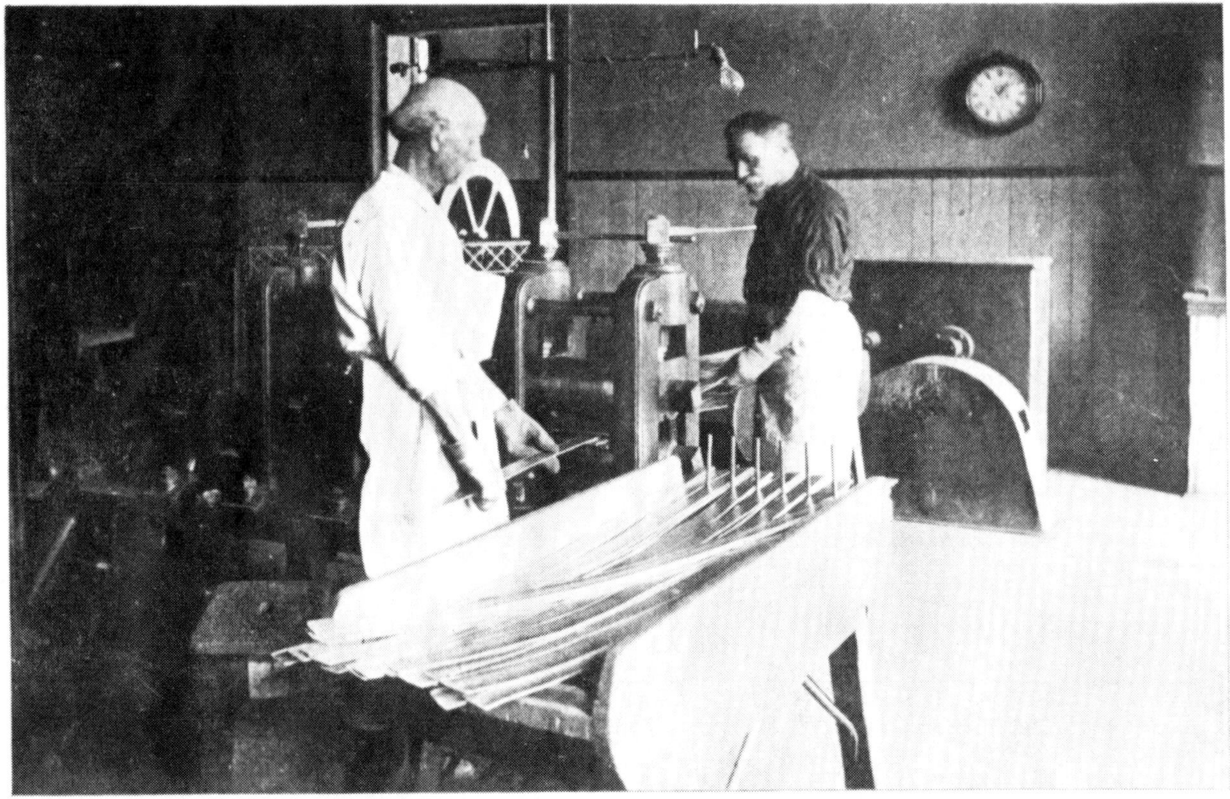

4. ROLLING THE STRIPS.

molds the ingots. You can see the open molds on the upper part of this machine which is made to revolve by means of the foot lever. When the lever is pressed down an arrangement at the back also closes one of the molds, which is then poured full of the melted silver. The lever is again pressed down, and the next mold is closed, etc. The machine is kept from getting too hot by a stream of cold water which is made to circulate on the inside of it. By the time three or four of the molds have been filled, the first ingot has, by the partial revolution, been brought around to the front, and is cool enough to be removed It is then released from its socket and drops into an iron box, where it is left to get cold. On a little truck in the fore-ground are a number of these boxes of ingots.

We followed our conductor back to a position in front of the big engine. Here are located the rolling machines. We were shown samples of the metal, as it is changed in form by the rollers. First the ingot, which I noticed is beveled off at one end in order that it may be more easily inserted between the rolls. Then a long strip which showed the result of passing the ingot nine times through the rollers. The ingot, being cast from melted metal, is hard to begin with; and after being rolled nine times the strip becomes so hard that it has almost a "spring" temper, and must be annealed before rolling further. The strips are placed in a furnace and heated red hot, then removed

5. PUNCHING OUT THE BLANKS.

and allowed to cool, which takes the temper out and softens the metal. After annealing, the strips are passed through the rolls fourteen times more, which reduces them to the proper thickness. The rolling has so drawn out and lengthened the strips (see Plate 4) that for convenience in handling they are next cut in two.

Having examined the work done by the rolling machines, we were conducted upstairs where we saw the next operation in dollar-making. By referring to Plate 5 you can see the machine which punches out the discs of metal called "blanks." Some of these blanks, however, are imperfect, and the good ones must be carefully sorted out. This is done on a table near by. The defective pieces, together with what remains of the strips after punching, are returned to the melting department.

After sorting, the good blanks are taken to the adjusting room, where women only are employed. We looked in upon them at their work. (Plate 6.) Very sensitive balances are used in this work, and the high degree of skill required in the various manipulations is surely a compliment to the women. Here the blanks are weighed first, to separate "lights" from "heavies." The standard weight of a perfect silver dollar is 412½ grains. In weighing the blanks, 1½ grains variation is allowed above or below the standard. After the light blanks are separated from the heavy, they are weighed again. Those that go

6. ADJUSTING DEPARTMENT.

above the limit of upper variation are filed off around the edge. Should too much filing be required, they are condemned. If the weight falls below the limit of lower variation, they are also condemned, and must be re-melted.

After the blanks are thus inspected they are sent to the "milling" room. In passing through the milling machine, the edge of the blank is evenly raised and smoothed, by being made to roll, in a horizontal plane, between two grooved surfaces, the space between which gradually diminishes. The raised edge is to protect the engraved portions of the coin from wear. After milling, the blanks are taken to the annealing furnace, heated red hot, then dipped in a weak solution of boiling hot sulphuric acid. This takes the temper out and cleans the silver. They are then dipped in clear cold water which rinses off the acid. After this they are placed in the drying machine, where they are rolled in hot saw-dust, which absorbs the moisture. The saw-dust is removed by rolling the coins in the screen cylinder, or "riddle," which is a part of the drying machine. (See left side Plate 8.) The blanks are now ready to receive the stamp and seal of the United States Government. The coining presses are located in a room by themselves, a general view of which may be seen in Plate 9. Here we see the lady attendant in position, feeding the press. On the stand at her elbow is a box of blanks. On the truck at the left are two trays of brand-new dollars. It is indeed an interesting sight to watch the shining pieces as they pass between

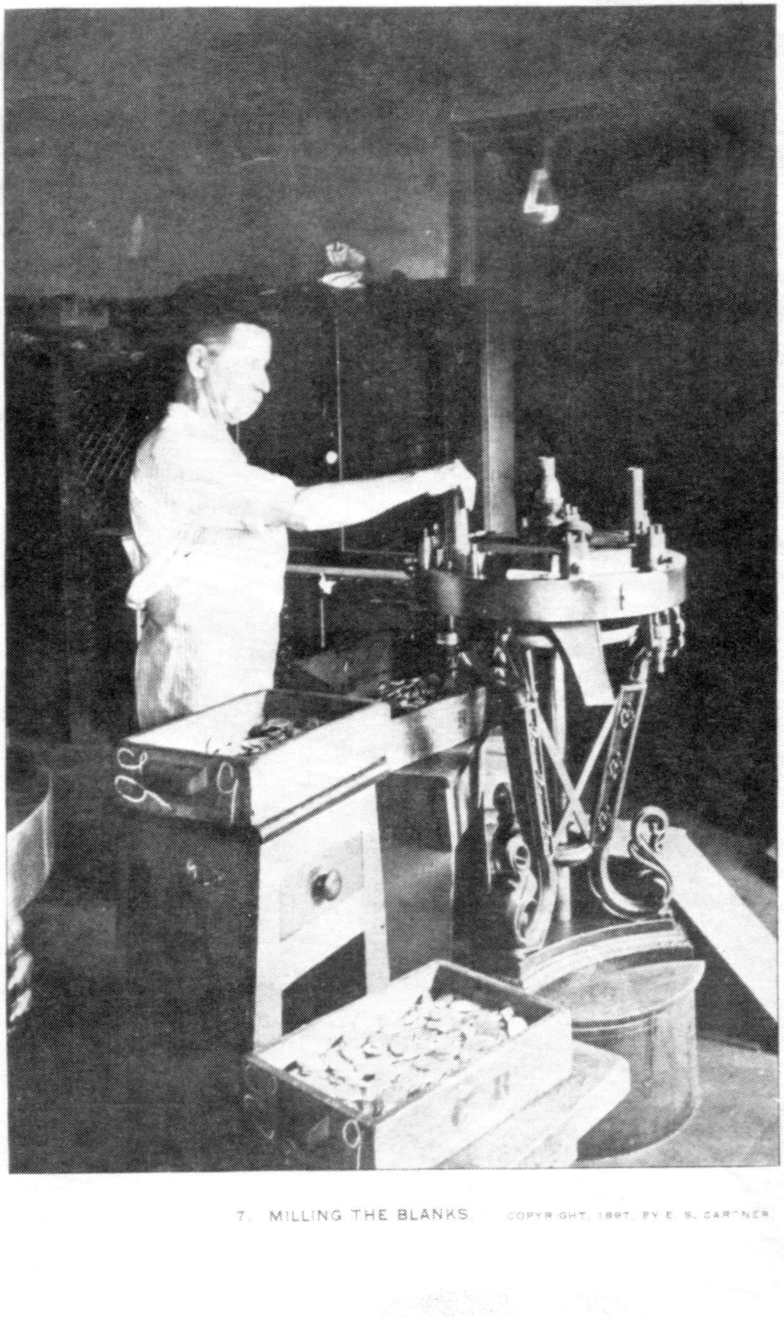

7. MILLING THE BLANKS.

the dies and receive the impressions which add so much to their appearance and value. The coining press is a very powerful machine; and yet one would hardly imagine that in the rapid and quiet movement, each descent of the die is backed by 150 tons pressure.

While we stand in fascinated admiration contemplating this magic money-maker, and hear the merry "clink" of the coins as they drop, at the average rate of 85 per minute, into the box beneath the press, the conductor has brought for our inspection, samples of the bright new dollars. They are indeed beauties! Each one is a work of art! Let us examine it closely. How perfect and realistic are the lines of the face and head, with the wreath and crown of "Liberty" of which we are all so proud! Above is the secret of our liberty, "E Pluribus Unum," and below are the stars representing our thirteen original States. If you look carefully on the lower edge of the neck you can see a little "M," which is the mark of the engraver of the dies, whose name is Morgan.

Let us reverse the coin. There is represented the American eagle, guardian spirit of our National liberty and honor. Note his position. With eye alert, and wings extended — every feather bristling with pride — he holds in his talons the emblems of Peace and War. The olive branch is held in advance of the arrows, indicating that we prefer to maintain our National liberty in peace, but if necessary we will defend it with the strong arm of war. Above the eagle's

8. ANNEALING AND CLEANING.

head, "In God we trust," a National tribute of our faith in Him "who doeth all things well." Just below the center of the ornamental wreath is a little "o," which is the mark of the New Orleans Mint.

As we return the coin to our friend, we feel that we have seen the dollar in a new and stronger light; and aside from the commercial use of its purchasing power, we shall ever regard it as a source of patriotic inspiration, and one of the fit emblems of a free people.

In Plate 10 we have a closer view of the most interesting part of the coining press, showing a blank ready to be coined, the face of the lower die, and a finished dollar beyond. When the press is in operation the lower die drops down so that when the blank is pushed forward by the sliding "feeders," it drops into its place immediately over the lower die and inside of a steel ring or "collar," which it loosely fits. On the inner edge of the collar are tooth-like projections, similar to those on a coarse file. When the upper die descends with its 150 tons pressure, the blank is so squeezed that it is made to expand in the direction of its edge. This expansion forces the silver against the fluted inner surface of the collar, and thus is formed the notched edge, or "reeding" (as it is called at the Mint), on the outer rim of the coin. When the pressure is released and the upper die is raised, the lower die raises also and forces the dollar up and out of the collar, from which position it is pushed out of the way and a new blank takes its place when the die descends again.

9. STAMPING ROOM.

When we consider the immense pressure brought to bear in stamping each one of these dollars, one would naturally think that the dies would soon wear out. I questioned our friend, the conductor, in regard to this, and he said that, on an average, a set of dies will coin about 350,000 silver dollars; sometimes more, according to how perfectly the dies have been tempered.

From the stamping room the dollars are taken back to the adjusting room, where each coin is examined separately and inspected for proper weight, appearance and sound. After this inspection, the dollars are taken to the "weigh" room for the Coiner's department (Plate 11), where they are first weighed in bulk and then counted. The conductor informed us that the large scales used in this department will weigh from 5,000 ounces down to *one grain*. A wonderfully fine adjustment for so large a balance.

In preparing for a "delivery," which usually consists of 1,000 dollars, the Assistant Coiner takes 500 "light" and 500 "heavy" dollars and places them on the scales. Should they weigh too much, he takes out a certain number of heavy and replaces them with the same number of light coins. In this manner the weight is brought within the allowed variation, which is only 2-100 of an ounce on 1,000 dollars.

On the table, we see in the center, an instrument made of wood, and shaped like a carpenter's square, except that its two sides are of equal length. This

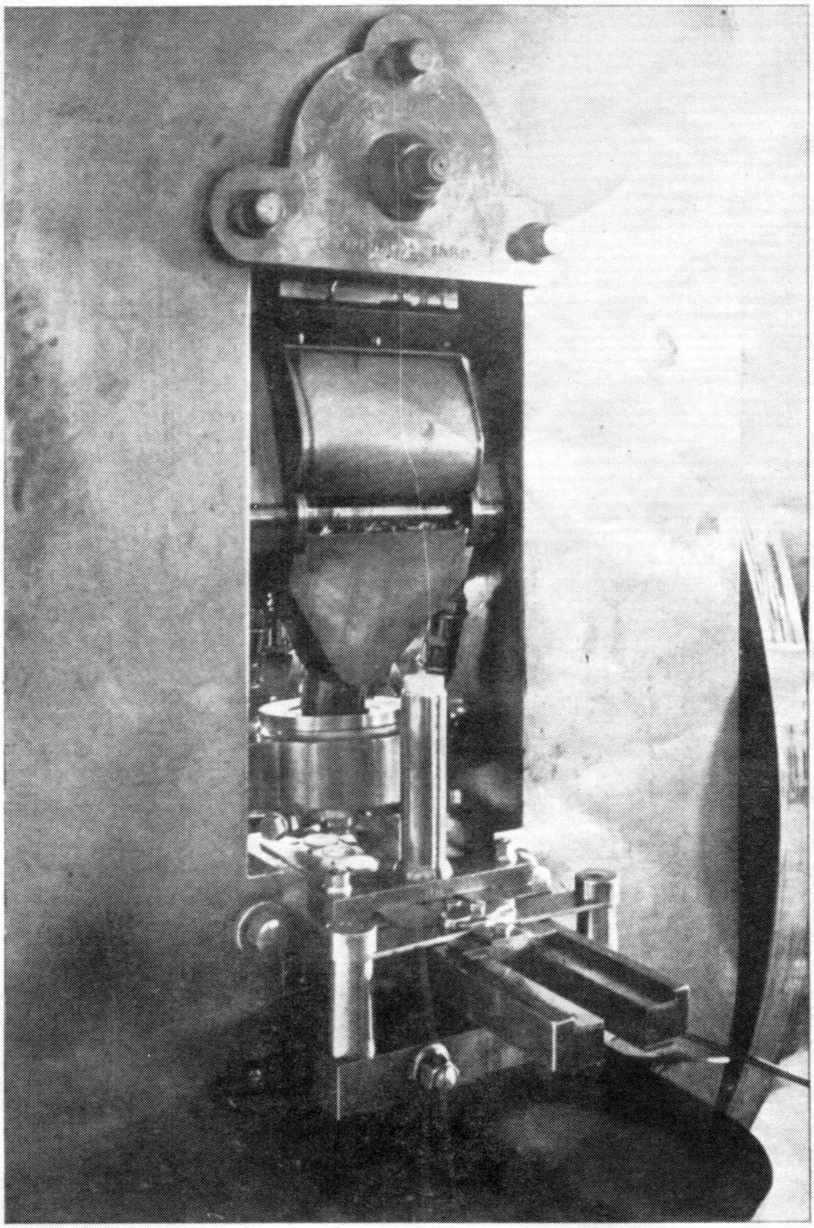

10. DETAIL OF STAMPING PRESS, SHOWING DIES.

instrument is used to quickly and accurately count the 1,000 dollars which constitute a delivery. Each pile, within the angle of this square, contains ten dollars, and there are ten piles in each row, and ten rows in the square. By this arrangement it would seem that there is no possibility of error, as the height of the wooden square corresponds exactly with the height of each pile, and the length of each of its inner sides is identical to the length of ten of the piles placed side by side.

After counting, the coins are ready for delivery. The Superintendent of the Mint is notified, and he sends his representative, who takes a position where he can see the indicator of the balance. If the weight of the 1,000 dollars should go above or below the 2-100 of an ounce allowed variation, the whole delivery is refused and must be counted over.

When the delivery is accepted by the Superintendent, the coins are placed in a vault to await the approval of the Assayer's Department at Washington.

A certain number of the coins are sent there to be tested for weight and fineness. If this inspection does not meet all requirements, the whole delivery is condemned, the local Assayer loses his position, and the whole lot has to be re-coined.

After approval by the Assayer's Department at Washington, the coins are ready for circulation, and are held subject to the order of the Sub-treasury.

11. WEIGHING AND COUNTING—COINER'S DEPARTMENT.

We have thus observed the last of the progressive operations in the coining of a silver dollar; and, as we follow our conductor back to the main entrance, we feel that our visit to the Mint has been a highly entertaining and profitable event, which we shall long remember with pleasure; and, as we journey on through future months and years, I dare say we will ever be watching our coins for the little "o," which is the mark of the New Orleans Mint.

In order that the reader may more readily review the principal operations in coinage, I have prepared, in Plate 12, a collection of samples showing the evolution of the dollar. At the top we have a brick of pure silver bullion. Under it a brick of pure copper. Next comes the ingot, which, as you will remember, contains 10 per cent of copper, making it "coin" silver. The dollar ingot averages 45 ounces in weight, is 14 inches long, $1\frac{3}{4}$ inches wide and $\frac{1}{2}$ inch thick. The plain strip shows the result of passing the ingot twenty-three times through the rolls. Next we see it perforated, showing where the blanks were punched out. In the blanks, next below the perforated strip, we have the first suggestion of a dollar. Next we notice the "milled" blanks. You can see where the edge has been raised. All these milled blanks, except the last one on the left, have passed through the acid-cleaning process. Notice the difference in color. The last row shows the stamped and finished dollars, of which about 600,000 per month are now being coined at this Mint. (April, 1897.)

12. EVOLUTION OF THE DOLLAR.

Coins of the United States now in circulation, with their weight and fineness, and amount coined to June 30, 1896.—*Taken from "Report of the Director of the Mint, 1896."*

	WEIGHT.	FINENESS.	TOTAL AMOUNT COINED TO JUNE 30, 1896.
GOLD COINS—	*Grains.*		
Double Eagle	516	.900	$1,277,693,220 00
Eagle	258	.900	266,538,270.00
Half Eagle	129	.900	220,631,035.00
Quarter Eagle	64.5	.900	28,711,015.00
SILVER COINS—			
Dollar	412.5	.900	$ 438,821,279.00
Half Dollar	192.9	.900	132,662,308.00
Columbian Half Dollar	192 9	.900	2,501,052.50
Quarter Dollar	96.45	.900	51,166,166 75
Columbian Quarter Dollar . . .	96.45	.900	10,005.75
Dime	38.58	.900	28,904,300.50

MINOR COINS.

FIVE CENT (NICKEL)—Weight, 77.16 grains; composed of 75 per cent copper and 25 per cent nickel; total amount coined to June 30, 1896 . . . . $14,292,235.30

CENT (BRONZE)—Weight, 48 grains; composed of 95 per cent copper and 5 per cent tin and zinc; total amount coined to June 30, 1896 . . . . 8,073,910.34

For more great history from the state of Louisiana, please visit the properties of the

Louisiana State Museum:

IN THE HISTORIC FRENCH QUARTER:

The Cabildo, 701 Chartres St., Jackson Square, New Orleans, La.

The Presbytere, 751 Chartres St., Jackson Square, New Orleans, La.

The Arsenal, 600 St. Peter St., Jackson Square, New Orleans, La.

Old U.S. Mint, 400 Esplanade Ave., New Orleans, La.

Madame John's Legacy, 632 Dumaine St., New Orleans, La.

The 1850 House. 523 St. Ann St., Jackson Square, New Orleans, La.

OUTSIDE OF NEW ORLEANS:

Wedell-Williams Aviation Museum (Louisiana State Museum - Patterson), 394 Airport Circle Road, Patterson, La.

Old Courthouse Museum (Louisiana State Museum - Natchitoches), 600 Second Street, Natchitoches, La.

E.D. White Historic Site, 2295 La. Hwy. 1, Thibodaux, La.

Louisiana State Museum - Baton Rouge, 660 N. Fourth Street, Baton Rouge, La.